Blogging
for
Profit

Learn How to Make Money Blogging With Step by Step Instruction

By Terence Lawfield

Published in Canada

© Copyright 2015 – Terence Lawfield

ISBN-13: 978-1507896716
ISBN-10: 1507896719

Table of Contents

Introduction

The Starting Point

We all have heard stories of six figure bloggers making a kill from their blogging activities. The internet is also filled with lots of absurd promises on how you can transform from an ordinary 8-5 working guy to an internet celebrity who tours the world as his or her blog makes him or her money on autopilot. In as much as some of these stories are true, there is a huge difference between those who hear the tales of these millionaire bloggers and those who actually become millionaire bloggers. This doesn't mean that those who don't make millions of dollars annually from blogging are losers; you don't have to make millions of dollars from blogging to be considered a success story.

This doesn't mean that making hundreds or thousands of dollars from blogging is any easier; in fact, you will be amazed that a vast majority of bloggers don't make any money from blogging. Many actually end up giving up blogging altogether while many of those who continue blogging never understand how they can monetize their blog leave alone driving traffic to the blog. So, what do you think would make your blog any different given that a new blog is established every half a second? You could easily end up getting lost deep in the volumes of other pages such that no one ever visits your site unless you give them the direct link to the blog then ask them to visit. With a new blog established every half a second, you need to do something that makes you stand out from the many others that end up not making any money. Irrespective of the niche you settle for, it is best to understand how to start and grow a money making blog. I will take you through a step by step process to help you transform your newly established blog or the blog you are thinking of establishing to a money making venture. Although the incomes will differ for different people based on different reasons, I assure you that you will make money when you follow this guide. Before going much further, let's first start with a short introduction about a blog.

What is a Blog?

A blog is a truncation coined from the expression weblog and is simply an informational or discussion website webhosts publish on the internet consisting of different entries or posts. When posting entries on a blog, these are usually displayed from the most recent post to the outdated ones in a reverse chronological order. While blogs developed today, usually include posts written and professionally edited by numerous authors, blogs developed before 2009 were usually the work of a single person, sometimes a small group, and were largely based on a single subject.

Today, you will often find multi author blogs from such media outlets as newspapers dominating blog traffic. You can also use a blog as a verb, that is, to add or maintain content in your blog. Before the emergence and development of blogs late in the 1990s, you needed to be conversant with both HTML and FTP in order to post anything on the web. However, since the introduction of web publishing tools that enable non-technical users to post content on the web, all you actually need is a good platform such as WordPress to create your own blog.

The best thing about blogs is that they are interactive and visitors can leave comments, reviews and even communicate with each other through graphical user interface widgets. This is the main difference between a blog and other static websites. As such, you can say that a blog is a kind of social networking service. This is especially true considering that apart from producing content on their blogs, bloggers also nurture social relations with their readers as well as with other bloggers. However, there are different types of blogs. Some high readership blogs like Daring Fireball don't allow comments, while most others provide commentary based on a specific topic. Some are more like online personal diaries while others serve as advertising platforms for a particular company or individual.

The basic features of a typical blog include images, text, and links to web pages, other blogs, and any other media related to the topic in question. The fact that readers can leave comments on a blog in an interactive format is what has led to the popularity of a majority of the blogs you see today.

While most blogs are mainly textual, there are exceptions that concentrate on art – art blogs, photographs - photoblogs, videos – video blogs, music – MP3 blogs and audio - podcasts. Other types of blogs include microblogging that feature very short posts, and edublogs that are used as instructional resources in education.

Although there are a few exceptions, generally, blogs usually have a few things in common:

*The main area of content where articles are displayed chronologically with the newest at the top
*An archive of previous articles
*A platform for visitors to leave comments
*Links to other websites and blogs related to the blog or topic at hand
*At least one "feed" such as Atom, RSS or PDF files

A blog isn't really complicated; you can start yours with little or no internet skills. Before you could even think of having a blog, you at least need to know what you want to blog about. The best place to start is to blog about something that you are passionate about otherwise you will easily lose interest when the money doesn't seem to be coming as quickly as you had thought.

How to Start a New Blog

Setting up a new blog is straightforward. You can do that in simple steps that won't even take more than 15 minutes:

*Search for a domain name (you can check them on Godaddy, Domize, iPage etc). Sub-domain names aren't all nice all the time so get your own domain. You should aim to have a blog with an address like *yourblog.com* and not *yourblog.subdomain.com*.

*Get a domain name and a hosting package (you can check at Hostgator ($3.49 per month), Bluehost ($6.95pm), Dreamhost ($8.95/ m)

Ensure that your preferred domain name is catchy, easy to remember and unique. Also, it is best to have a domain name comprising of keywords of the kind of stuff your blog is about. A domain name should cost you about $10 annually.

*Choose the blogging platform (Wordpress is the best place to start but you can choose any of the others including Blogger, Tumblr). Choose Wordpress.org if you want to go for a self-hosted blog (with your domain name); Wordpress.com is too basic and has limited capabilities especially in terms of making money. So, if you want to implement all the monetization options I will discuss shortly, you need to have a self hosted blog.

When you set everything up, the next phase is to customize the blog in a way that makes it easy to navigate, attractive and more user friendly just to mention a few of the essential characteristics of a good blog. You can buy a premium theme or use a free theme on your blog; a theme really spells how your blog will look like and how you will be able to navigate through it. The themes are also SEO optimized so you don't have to do much work after buying them; they come out of the box.

Premium themes are the best since they come with greater customization options than free ones. This should cost you anywhere between $50 and $100. Once you are comfortable with the way your blog looks like (don't worry, you can always tweak it to your liking), you can now publish your first blog post. Just to get you up to speed on what will make the difference between you and everyone else who ends up disappointed with the idea of blogging; you need to follow a few unwritten rules if you are to emerge successful.

Quality sells

You have to produce high quality relevant content irrespective of the purpose of your blog. No one would come visiting your site frequently when you are constantly posting crap on your page. Think of it as a musician who is constantly making poor quality music that doesn't rest well with the audience; do you think people would be willing to continue buying leave alone listen to their music?

Build the platform

Blogging isn't just about making you direct income; you can think of it as advertising space where you put yourself to the rest of the world for them to gauge your skills, ideas and other aspects. This could be a great platform to springboard yourself towards greater business besides just blogging.

Relationship building

Don't just hide behind blog posts and not connect with your readers. It is best to connect with them so that they know the guy behind the brilliant ideas or perspectives.

Diversify your income

A blog has endless possibilities on how it brings money. In any case, it is a shop which has opened its doors for anyone from anywhere in the world to come shopping even if it is just for information. Use that platform to diversify your income streams from the blog. So, how exactly can you make money from the blog? I will take you through various ways through which you can generate money from your blog.

With all that in mind, the next step phase is to set up your blog in a way that enables you to make money from it. This is known as monetization. You can set up your blog to bring in multiple income streams. In the next section, I will show you how you can use some creative ways to monetize your blog so that you can start making real money from your blogging efforts.

Chapter 1:
Monetizing Your Blog When Starting

While there are several ways to make money from your blog, it is essential to evaluate the nature or purpose of the blog before diving fully into it to ensure that you tap into every possible revenue source. Unfortunately, most people tend to give up too early after a couple of setbacks. It takes time before you can actually start earning a tidy income from blogging, but once you start, it's a walk in the park. Below is a compilation of some of the things you can do to start earning from your weblog. I have classified them into easy (beginner) blogger monetization options and intermediary/advanced monetization options. The beginner tips will enable you to start making money right away when you start the blog while the intermediary or advanced tips need you to have a fairly established blog to make money.

Advertising

One of the most popular ways of making money with a blog is through advertising. You can do that in different ways namely:

Advertising networks
All you have to do is sign up with a network and then copy paste an ad code from the network website to your blog to avail your ad spaces. From there, you just designate a space on your blog where you want the ads to appear. Advertisers will then bid for your ad spaces by means of a real time auction. The ad that pays the most will then show on your blog. In most cases, the network website will handle the payment directly, and then pay you in turn. Most bloggers prefer Google Adsense, but there are several other alternatives like Sovrn, Rivit, Sway, Media.net, BurstMedia, BlogHer, Chitika, Blogads, Beacon Ads, Federated Media. and Kontera. You can check some more on WAHAdventures.

These advertising networks usually operate on a CPM (Click Per Impression) or Pay Per Click basis. This means that the income you will generate will vary from month to month based on the number of validated clicks you have had.

Some of the factors you should consider when looking for an advertising network include:

*Whether the network is registering new bloggers, or if it is by invite only

*The requirements for joining the network (profanity, frequency of posting, traffic, etc)

*Whether they require individuality – i.e. can you run other ad networks or ads?

*Whether they allow paid (sponsored) posting

*Positioning of ad banners – do you have to place their ad banner at the top of your blog in order for it to count impressions?

*Their payments – normally it is expressed as X dollars per CPM

*Their clients – whether they are little businesses or fortune 500 companies

*Whether they run plenty of filler and public service advertisements

*Whether you can control the adverts – i.e. is it possible for you to opt out of a campaign if you are not interested in dealing with the advertiser?

*The media outlets partnering with the ad network

Tip: the position of ads on your blog have a profound effect on the number of valid clicks that you actually end up having so ensure that you master the best ad placement spots. You can do that by experimenting with different ad positions until you find the best spot where the ads receive the highest clicks.

Direct ad sales (Private ads)

A direct advertising sale is simply designating a space in your blog to advertise someone else's products or services, usually in the form of a text or image link. The best thing about direct advertising sales is that you get to keep one hundred percent of the profit, and in some cases your blog doesn't need to have plenty of traffic for you to start earning (depending on your market). Even if you start by making 5 dollars per month, this is enough to pay for your hosting and to build the much-needed confidence that you can actually make money from blogging.

You can decide to either charge based on impressions, which are usually set at per thousand impressions (CPM – cost per impression), or you could set a flat price on a monthly basis. For instance, if an advertisement has a CPM rate of $4, then you would earn $400 for a hundred thousand impressions. Once you have determined the size of the space you want to use for advertising and the costs, proceed to look for businesses and friends who might be interested in advertising on your blog. Local and small businesses are a great place to start. Having real adverts on your blog goes a long way in showing people that you are selling your ad space and that people are using it.

Affiliate Marketing

Another great way to make money with your blog if you are a starter is through affiliate marketing. This is basically advertising someone else's products or services and then getting paid a commission for all purchases made by your referrals. The good thing about this is that you don't need to care much about storing or delivering of such products since everything is done by the seller; your work is to tell people that the seller is selling a certain product then you get paid.

However, since this works on a commission basis, the visitor has to click on the ad or link, and then sign up for something before you can get paid. The commission will vary, depending on the products. Some sites will even pay you a commission even if the person doesn't buy the specific product whose link you provided but anything else; provided that they used your link. So, what affiliate program should you sign up for to monetize your blog?

The best approach here is to join affiliate programs that are directly associated with your particular niche. For example, if your blog is focused on photography, you could become an affiliate with a particular camera equipment dealer. A good program to start with if you are a beginner is Amazon Associates, which sells millions of different products so you are more likely to find a fit for your blog. Amazon Associates can pay up to 5 percent for movies and music, and 8.5 percent for kindle books.

Affiliate links can prove to be a great source of income, if used right. Be sure to inform your readers that there are instances where you may be prompted to use affiliate links. While you should focus on affiliate programs that are directly related to your niche, you can always be on the lookout for different types of products that can interest your audience. ClickBank is another popular site where you can make a lot of money in form of affiliate commissions.

Other popular sites that work with affiliates include Affiliate Network, Affiliate Window, Rakuten Affiliate Network (formerly Linkshare), CJ Affiliate (formerly commission junction), Shareasale, Avangate, and ebaypartnernetwork just to mention a few.

Paid posts and sponsored reviews

Advertisers are always on the lookout for ways to promote their goods and services. One good way for them to increase their sales is through reviews posted in different blogs. Sponsored reviews are simply reviews about a certain product or service that you have written for a fee. As a starter, you probably want to start by writing short, perfectly edited and well formatted blogs for other people before you can draw some audience to your own blog. A paid blog, on the other hand, is an article that someone else has written and wants you to advertise it for a fee on your blog.

While both sponsored reviews and paid posts can generate quite a good amount of money, paid posts can turn out to be a poorly written article. However, the good thing is that all you have to do with paid posts is to copy paste the article to your blog and click publish. As you gain more visitors on your blog, advertisers are more likely to approach you about paid posts and sponsored reviews more frequently.

Tip: The best approach is to test them with your readers, but be sure to leave a disclaimer that the post is an ad; otherwise, your audience may wrongly assume that you are the one who wrote the article.

As I already mentioned, it is possible to implement some tips during the beginning phase but as for others, it is easier to implement them when your blog has some content and some steady traffic (it doesn't matter how much traffic). In the next section, I will show you how to make more money as your blog enters the development stage.

Chapter 2:
Monetizing Your Blog in the
Development Stage

Selling Products and Services

As your blog grows and gains more followers, it is bound to generate more traffic. As such, this makes it the perfect platform to launch products and services. There are ideally two things to consider when selling products and services on your blog.

For starters, selling products for one is much harder than selling services, as the former requires plenty of creativity and hard work. People are more willing to exchange ideas rather than buy products from a blog.

Secondly, if you decide to be an exclusive retail blogger, it is obvious that the main topic of discussion in your blog will be a single agenda: your product. If you want to capture the attention of your audience and get them to buy your product, you need to understand that people are more inclined to buy new products based on a particular story. Therefore, you need to link your product with a compelling story to make it more convincing. You can create compelling stories using short guest posts, amateur videos, and customer photos. If your blog has a focused traffic, it can generate a huge amount of money for you by selling products to your readers directly.

Some popular products you can sell include courses, t-shirts, books, membership websites, and accessories. The product has a higher probability of selling with more readers on your blog, as long as it is related to your blog's subject. To get some ideas of some of the things you could sell to your blog's visitors, visit some similar blogs that are within your niche and find out what they are selling.

Additionally, you could generate income from your blog by marketing services. However, keep in mind that selling services requires a practically different approach from that of selling a product. While the former involves convincing your audience that they need or want the product you are offering (which is a pretty subjective issue), the latter involves convincing your clients that you are an expert in your particular profession or niche. Some of the services you could sell include consultancy, freelancing, one on one coaching etc. Your blog should be a platform for promoting the experience you have and marketing yourself.

There are plenty of folks out there willing to pay for your time and knowledge, so take advantage and make some money out of it.

Good examples of how you can make this work are as follows:

Write an eBook

Since most people are doing it anyway, it does not hurt to give it a try. With the introduction of such commercial e-readers as Amazon Kindle and iPad, these have become especially popular over the last few years. The book could be about anything, like a DIY for renovating a house, as long as it is useful to people. You can then publish it on Amazon or Apple iStore, or sell it on your blog directly. The best part of selling directly from your blog is that you get 100 percent of the overall sale price and attract traffic to your blog in the process.

Write a hardback book

This is also applicable if you have written an eBook. If you are a good writer, you can publish a paperback or hardback version and sell it on your blog. However, you have more chances of succeeding in this approach if you have an existing audience. On the other hand, you can also create a blog based on a successful book to promote it on an international scale. It can work both ways. This is a great option especially for good writers, and you can even use a self-publishing website like iUniverse to publish your own book.

Write guides and tutorials

The internet is undoubtedly the greatest source of information. People use the internet to look for tutorials on how to do almost anything. You are reading a guide on how to earn money from your blog right this moment! Perhaps you are not so knowledgeable when it comes to cars. You can find several useful guides and tutorials explaining technical things about cars that you do not know. You probably know something that you can teach someone else, so why don't you write it and post it in your blog. If the niche you are writing about is particularly popular, chances are you could attract plenty of traffic to your blog.

Teaching program

After writing a tutorial on a particular subject, you can take this opportunity to create your very own online teaching course. People can then pay a membership fee or a fixed charge for joining the course you have established. The courses could be about any topic and can include tutorials, videos, podcasts, and so on. If you are an expert in photography for instance, you could organize a two week training course on how to be a great photographer. In addition, you could also make videos explaining all the equipments you might need, how to take shots in a dark room, techniques on how to take excellent photos, etc.

However, just make sure the information you charge your paying audience is relatively genuine and different from that, which is freely available on your blog otherwise, you will receive countless complaints for charging overwhelmingly high prices for information that is just free in your blog.

Be a consultant

Another great way to make money using your blog is by providing consultation services within your specific niche. The challenge is that you need to have a large following as well as a good reputation in your field of expertise for you to earn money using this method.

For a fixed rate, you can offer consultation services on a one on one basis to people via Skype or even over the phone. People are more likely to pay for this service as they are gaining from your undivided attention. For example, if you are an expert in health and fitness with a great reputation, you may offer a consultation fee for a service where people can arrange to engage with you via a web cam. You can even charge an all time 100 dollars for the hour and the person may not need to contact you any time soon. However, you may need to reconsider using this method if your blog is relatively new. More established bloggers make lots of money from this.

Email Marketing

Email marketing is one of the most effective methods of reaching a particular audience, regardless of whether you want to sell goods and services, deliver info services, build relationships or attain any other goal. One thing that makes email marketing effective is the fact that there is a lot of trust put on the messages we permit there.

Email marketing works by simply providing an opt-in form to your readers where they can fill in their email addresses. This way, you can nurture a mutual relationship with them by providing consistent value. The two most used email-marketing tools are Aweber and GetResponse.

Email marketing allows you to deliver your message instantly when advertising some given information directly to the inboxes of your email subscribers. I would recommend you start creating your email lists immediately, rather than waiting for your blog to grow. This way, you can use all the monetization techniques discussed here so far. You need to master how to write good email copies to increase conversions. This could be done through using ethical techniques that will minimize the number of emails that end up in the spam folders of your email subscribers.

Audio Advertising

You may not have considered this yet, but Pay Per Play can make you a significant amount of money. These are audio adverts, which only last a few seconds and are played each time someone visits your blog. In most cases, you can make up to $5 dollars for every unique visitor, but this method is very intrusive and can prove to be a turn off to your visitors.

Podcast adverts are also great for advertising. If you run a weekly podcast for that matter updating your listeners about new information on your blog, then you could consider advertising as well. This is a less intrusive method since the podcast would appear like a radio show with short commercial breaks. This is a great way to monetize your blog, as long as you do not get ahead of yourself with the amount of advertisements.

Pop Ups

You have probably heard or seen these, as they are very common on the internet. However, these can also be annoying. In fact, most people hate them so much that they even install pop-up blockers to stop them. Nevertheless, if you execute them in the right way, you can make money out of them. For instance, if have only one pop up that appears only to new visitors to your blog, it can work in your favor.

You don't necessarily have to sell anything directly with pop-ups. You can use them to promote a certain aspect of your blog indirectly. PopUp Domination, for example, can be used to promote new signings to your email list of a certain tutorial course. As long as people do not find them annoying, pop-ups can work to your advantage.

Text Link Ads

This form of advertising normally involves including text based adverts within your articles. If you are writing an article on software X, you can incorporate text link ads in your article to refer your readers to that software. However, you will need to sign up with Software X affiliate advertising scheme or a specialized service provider who will then automate the service. One good service to use is matomyseo, as it provides a non-intrusive method of making money without pissing off your readers.

Marketplace/Classifieds/Job Board

As you develop more traffic, more and more doors will start opening up to you. You can take advantage of this traffic by launching a dedicated marketplace, job board or classifieds. The good news is that these are easy to set up and they provide a platform for people to buy and sell stuff, as well as to advertise. When your marketplace becomes successful, you can then charge a fee for posting ads. One great tool to use to create your very own marketplace is sharetribe.

Sell Your Blog

When all is said and done, you can always sell your blog for a profit. If your personal circumstances change, and you find that you need more time or money (or both), you can simply sell your blog and make some good money. Several factors are put into consideration when a potential buyer puts a price on your blog. However, income is the most overwhelming influence on the final selling price.

If you are making money from your blog, you will have buyers lining up to bid for your blog. On the other hand, if you are not making anything from your blog, chances are you are the one who will be wasting time looking for people to bid. Therefore, the best time to sell your blog is as soon as it has become profitable.

Chapter 3:
Practical Tips on How to Make the Most Money as a Blogger

When embarking on a blogging career, the most important thing to keep in mind is patience. While most people do not consider blogging as a suitable means of income, leave alone a career, it is a field that is dominated by thousands of people who make a living out of it – a good one for that matter. Blogging is a profession, like any other. However, the learning never stops. If you want to achieve a consistent income from blogging, here are a few tips to help you get started:

Use your ad space wisely

While selling ads is lucrative since it is a passive income, you can actually make 3 to 10 times more selling your own products and services on that same space, or even advertise an affiliate product.

Start from reverse

When companies want to introduce a certain product in the market, they start by giving out freebies, then they offer you a cheap but irresistible product, and then they finally lure you into buying a much more expensive item. This is a tried and successful marketing tactic, which you should use in your blog, but start in reverse in this case. For instance, if you want to sell an eBook, you are much more likely to be frustrated if you start with a cheap eBook.

The reason for this is that the real profit lies not at the beginning of the funnel, but at the end. Of course, selling eBooks is great if you have a few other expensive products to sell afterwards. But it is a downright stupid idea if you do not. It is much wiser to start with the expensive product first, and then get down to the cheaper ones. If you have cheaper products to sell, you can offer these to your new audience for starters, keeping in mind that you have more profitable items to sell them later.

"Cheap" markets do not exist

Even with a following of 1 million subscribers, chances are your customers cannot afford to buy a $10,000 product, unless of course you are dealing with multimillionaires. In fact, most of your customers will not be able to pay for premium products, but the interesting part is that it does not matter.

In most cases, you can make much more money selling to the minority than you could ever make with the vast majority. For example, if you want to sell a yearlong training course for writers that cost roughly ten thousand dollars, you can actually fill the vacancies within minutes after opening the course. Here is why: if you notify forty thousand writers about the course, two percent of the group might possibly be willing to pay for the product in that price range, which makes about 800 people.

You might decide to accept only ten people to fill the vacancies, by which you will be creating a scenario of extreme scarcity. You can do this with an even smaller number. For example, if you have a support base of one hundred subscribers, two of them could actually afford your premium products or services, and those two could often pay much more than the rest of your customers combined.

Evaluate your time

The value of the activities you do will actually depend on your goal. For example, if you are aiming to increase traffic to your blog, start measuring the amount of time you invest looking for visitors. Let's say that you spend 3 hours writing an article and it attracts one hundred visitors, and another 5 hours writing a guest article that attracts five hundred visitors. Writing your own article in this case brings you roughly thirty three visitors per hour, while the guest article brings you around one hundred visitors per hour. As such, you are better off using your time guest posting rather than writing for your own blog.

Don't rush into writing your own content

Think of your blog as an empty classroom, with you as the teacher all by yourself. Of course, you may decide to give a lecture, but even if it is the best lecture that has ever been given, it is useless when no one is around to listen. It won't really matter since no one else heard it. As such, when starting out, writing content for your blog is relatively inefficient when it comes to building traffic.

It is far much wiser to spend your time writing guest posts for another blogger's audience and impress the hell out of them. This way, you can then portion out a part of the readership to your own blog. Start accumulating email subscribers as a guest in other people's blogs so that you can at least have an audience to present your content as soon as you start posting entries.

Take advantage of webinars

One of the most underutilized ways you can use to make money from blogging is webinars. Most people are unaware of this, but you can actually make serious cash from even a single webinar, and attract numerous email subscribers while you are at it. With this method, you can either conduct a webinar for someone else, or promote a product, either of which is guaranteed to bring in some good money.

Use longer but quality content

Regardless of the nature and size of the blog, longer content tends to attract more traffic than a shorter one. This means creating content between 2,000 and 3,000 words for every post. While it is true that longer content can consume much of your time, if you estimate the number of visitors it will bring you, I'd say it's worth the shot.

Promote the hell out of your content

While the key to monetizing a blog is essentially to promote it through vigorous ways, the problem is that most bloggers do not make enough effort to do this. Promotion here does not just mean sharing your blog posts on Facebook and Twitter. It means building relationships and connections with influencers and having them share your content through blogger outreach. At the very least, the time you spend creating content should equal the amount of time you spend on outreach.

Don't worry about SEO in the first year

Of course, SEO is a great way to draw traffic to your blog. However, it becomes a problem when you start concentrating on it way too early. Here, it all boils down to time. As a beginner blogger, the most important things that should eat up most of your time fall into three main categories: creating excellent content worth reading, nurturing relationships and connections with influencers, and selling products and services. Generally, if you hit the nail on the head on these three areas, you will not attract prominence and traffic, but your blog will also rank better on search results without doing anything.

Nurture your email list like your own child

In everything we do in life, there is always one factor that determines the success or failure of a given project; in analytics, it is known as OMTM (the one metric that matters). In blogging, it is the number of subscribers in your email list. Email marketing is one of the most effective methods of online marketing. Of course, the number alone does not matter when not utilized, but you can accurately predict your sales judging primarily by the size of your email list. For example, if you have an email list of about 2,000 people, you can assign one dollar for every subscriber in terms of sales. Therefore, 2,000 subscribers would result in $2,000 per month, 20,000 subscribers would mean $20,000 and so forth. You have to measure the value of your email list first before you can get to a point of estimating how much each subscriber is worth.

Start selling from the first day

When starting a blog, several things need to be put into consideration. Like a manufacturing industry, when one aspect of your blog seems to be lagging behind, it can cost you plenty of cash. In this case, the lagging factor is you assuming you are not conversant with the technical stuff of owning a blog. Therefore, this can prove to be a stubborn bottleneck to the growth of your blog, unless you can afford to hire someone else to handle all the technical details while you concentrate on the rest of the work.

As such, the best way to fully utilize your blog and your time is to start selling immediately so that you can start earning as soon as possible. However, do not make your blog a huge sale pitch, otherwise, you will not sale anything. Instead, start by offering your audience something they want or need but do not push it. You can always make it available and then remind them occasionally that they can buy it.

People will not always like your product ideas

When starting, you probably have a list of items on your mind that you can sell, no doubt. Whether it is eBooks, t-shirts, shoes, you name it. Here is the shocker; no one gives a single damn about your ideas. In fact, everyone else's ideas suck when viewed from another person's perspective, mine included. Creative people tend to create products that they see a certain targeted audience needs, but they are not actually aware of it. You keep thinking that if you can convince them of the magnitude of their problems, then they would consider buying your product or service to solve this problem but here is some more bad news; unless you are Steve Jobs, let's just say this is simply not going to work.

You are a starter blogger, and as such, you should be concentrating on selling products that will solve the problems your clientele is already aware of. If you have to convince your customers that the problem is there, you have already lost the battle!

Don't quit your day job yet

Blogging is hard work; you shouldn't expect to become an overnight millionaire in a day's or week's work. Keep your job until you are sure that the blog can bring in enough money from multiple streams to cater for your family needs.

Don't put your eggs in one basket

As a rule of thumb, you just cannot rely on a single revenue stream in your blog. A lot can change overnight so you have to be fully prepared by diversifying in other revenue streams if you want to be certain about your income.

Develop a blogging routine

The best way to sustain traffic from your audience is to have a blogging routine. It will also make you remain consistent in your blogging activities and even create more content; the web is driven by content remember!

Consistency and willingness to learn will take you very far in your blogging efforts.

All I have written could sound quite easy. However, when you don't know how to choose a niche and survive the turbulence that is in the blogging business world, you might easily get lost in between.

When choosing a niche:

*Don't just make it about yourself; instead, meet the needs of others. This is the best way to make real money from blogging. Choose something that you are passionate about too.

*Don't be too rigid about things; change with changing times if you want to survive. In this case, try out different tricks for monetizing your blog. Your audience might not like some of the things you are posting or the way you do certain things; for the sake of your audience, you need to change accordingly. In any case, they bring food on your table!

*Let the niche you settle for blend well with your personality. This will make it easy to continue publishing new blog posts even when you are not making a lot of money (you might be one among millions who make any money in their first week or month of blogging).

Even with the endless possibilities on how to start and monetize your blog, you still need to drive traffic to the blog to make that kind of money. In any case, millions of other blogs are started every year. How can you make sure that you can start generating traffic to your blog and not be one of the many that no one visits? You cannot teach an empty class or sell anything to no one!

Chapter 4:
How to Drive Traffic to Your Blog

These don't need much explanation since the names are pretty much straight forward

Guest posting: You can post in someone else's blog as a guest poster then leave a link pointing to your blog. Those impressed by your writing will probably click on the link to know more about you.

Commenting on forums: Participate in forums then ensure that you set your account to post with a signature pointing to your blog. The more value you add by posting high quality posts, the easier it would be to attract traffic to your blog.

Blog commenting: Start commenting on blogs that allow you to leave a link pointing back to your blog. You will be amazed that people will often want to check out what your blog has to offer.

Be part of blog community sites: The more you interact with other bloggers, the more you will get referral traffic from them hence more growth for your blog.

Submit your blog to blogcarnival.com: This one provides an avenue for publishing some of your best posts so that others can check them out outside your blog. You will be amazed by the amount of traffic that this option can bring.

Join various directories: Just Google "name of topic followed by directories" then try to register to as many of them as possible (read some reviews about the directories first). Some popular directories include blogged.com, dmoz.org, Dir.yahoo.com and botw.org just to mention a few.

Submit articles to article directories: As the name suggests, you just need to create an account in different article directories then publish an article. When publishing article, you can then leave a link pointing to your blog. Popular directories include goarticles.com, ezinearticles.com and articledashboard.com among many others.

Engaging your audience on social media: You need to know that social media is here to stay so you need to share whatever new content you publish in as many social media sites as possible. In any case, if you cannot beat it, join it! Sharing your content on Pinterest is particularly great if you are serious about attracting people who are ready to buy something. In this case, all your posts MUST have catchy photos to make people want to pin them. This doesn't mean that you should overlook the other social media sites in your efforts.

Now that you have everything you need to know to succeed as a blogger, it is time to start your blog today!